CH00405637

Distilling

poems for reflection and meditation

edited by Alison Morgan and Martin Cavender

"I'm discovering that a spiritual journey is a lot like a poem. You don't merely recite a poem or analyze it intellectually. You dance it, sing it, cry it, feel it on your skin and in your bones. You move with it and feel its caress. It falls on you like a teardrop or wraps around you like a smile. It lives in the heart and the body as well as the spirit and the head."

Sue Monk Kidd

"Not everything has a name. Some things lead us into the real beyond words... It is like that small mirror in the fairy-tales... You glance in it and what you see is not yourself; for an instant you glimpse the Inaccessible, where no horse or magic carpet can take you. And the soul cries out for it."

Alexander Solzhenitsyn

Collection © 2012 Alison Morgan and Martin Cavender

Copyright of individual poems and images rests with the authors and other rights holders as cited in the acknowledgements at the back of this book, which constitute an extension of this copyright page.

All rights reserved. No part of this publication may be reproduced, stored in a retrieval system, or transmitted in any form or by any means, electronic, mechanical, photocopying, recording or otherwise, without the prior written permission of the copyright owners.

Design and layout by Alison Morgan
Copyright research Paula Smit and Alison Morgan

We gratefully acknowledge the permission granted to reproduce the copyright material in this book. Every effort has been made to trace copyright holders and to obtain their permission for the use of the material. We apologise for any errors or omissions and would be grateful to be notified of any corrections that should be incorporated in future reprints or editions of this book.

The Bible translation on p76 is taken from the New Revised Standard Version of the Bible, Anglicized edition, copyright © 1989, 1995 by the Division of Christian Education of the National Council of the Churches of Christ in the United States of America, and is used by permission. All rights reserved.

ISBN 978-1-906363-36-9

Published by:
ReSource
13 Sadler Street, Wells, Somerset BA5 2RR
office@resource-arm.net
www.resource-arm.net
Charity no. 327035

September 2012

Foreword

Those of us who love poetry find that when we read it no solutions appear to the challenges of the day, no answers fall out of the air and land neatly on the page, and nothing tangible springs up from the sofa into our relationships. And yet always it seems that something shifts inside us, as if the poem were pouring invisible oil onto the wrinkled surface of our lives. Aristotle understood this; entering into the emotions, reflections, suffering even of others seems to cleanse something in our own souls. Why it should be so we are not sure; but we are convinced that poetry slows us down, helps us to pause over the desires and feelings that we so hastily suppress, and invites us to experience life in a way which is a little less predictable, a little less demanding than so often seems to be the case. Jesus, we may remind ourselves, dealt more often in metaphor than he did in fact; for facts close things down, but metaphors open them up. And therein lies life.

Poetry has the ability, paradoxically, not just to open things up but also to distil them. Jesus came to bring us life 'in all its fullness', and he spoke the word in poetry and imagination, grace and truth. There is something organic about this – in the words of John Keats, 'If poetry comes not as naturally as the leaves to a tree it had better not come at all.' The American writer Katherine Anne Porter observed 'Writing does not exclude the full life. It demands it.'

So, here is the full life through the words of poets, Christian and not, known and unknown, over 26 centuries. It all fits with the vision of the fragile but determined little initiative 'ReSource' for which we work. It is both about the reconnection with the source of our being and about being re*source*d, washed again in the streams of living water, the Holy Spirit who brings us life. This full life is about cleansing, renewal and healing; and that is the spirit in which we offer this book – with our thanks to so many people, five loaves and two fishes to be blessed and to provide food for the journey.

Alison Morgan   *Martin Cavender*

Alison Morgan and Martin Cavender
ReSource, Wells, September 2012

Contents

Distilling life

God's Dream

The Lord God said: I myself will dream a dream within you,
        Good dreaming comes from me, you know.
My dreams seem impossible,
            not too practical
            nor for the cautious man or woman;
            a little risky sometimes,
            a trifle brash perhaps.
Some of my friends prefer
                to rest more comfortably
                    in sounder sleep,
                    with visionless eyes.
But from those who share my dreams
            I ask a little patience,
            a little humour,
            some small courage,
            and a listening heart –
I will do the rest.

Then they will risk
            and wonder at their daring;
Run, and marvel at their speed;
Build, and stand in awe at the beauty of their building.

You will meet me often as you work
                in your companions who share the risk,
            in your friends who believe in you enough
                    to lend their own dreams,
                    their own hands,
                    their own hearts,
                        to your building.
In the people who will stand in your doorway,
            stay awhile
            and walk away knowing that they too can find a dream.
There will be sun-filled days
            and sometimes it will rain –

a little variety –
both come from me.

So come now, be content.
It is my dream you dream,
my house you build,
my caring you witness;
my love you share
And this is the heart of the matter.

Charles Péguy

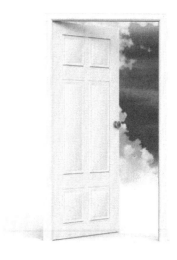

This Poem...

This poem is dangerous: it should not be left
Within the reach of children, or even of adults
Who might swallow it whole, with possibly
Undesirable side-effects. If you come across
An unattended, unidentified poem
In a public place, do not attempt to tackle it
Yourself. Send it (preferably, in a sealed container)
To the nearest centre of learning, where it will be rendered
harmless, by experts. Even the simplest poem
May destroy your immunity to human emotions.
All poems must carry a Government warning. Words
Can seriously affect your heart.

Elma Mitchell

I thank you God

i thank You God for most this amazing
day:for the leaping greenly spirits of trees
and a blue true dream of sky;and for everything
which is natural which is infinite which is yes

(i who have died am alive again today,
and this is the sun's birthday;this is the birth
day of life and of love and wings:and of the gay
great happening illimitably earth)

how should tasting touching hearing seeing
breathing any – lifted from the no
of all nothing – human merely being
doubt unimaginable You?

(now the ears of my ears awake and
now the eyes of my eyes are opened)

e.e.cummings

Open and Fastened

Opened and fastened, the empty satchel, so often,
The fabric is torn and the luminous plastic broken.
Small children are learning to be important.
One of them notices raindrops hitting the lane
Splash up, rimmed with knobs like a little crown.
He tells his teacher this; she says Sit down.

Unable to bear the thought of this taming I want
To lie on the hill in the rain and drown
Every instilled importance. Be flattened down
As the grass on the hill is bent white by the rain
That bounces the lane of the airy terrapin
Building the puzzled children fasten, unfasten empty satchels in.

P J Kavanagh

Rag and Bone

That sun ray has raced to us
at those millions of miles an hour.
But when it reaches the floor of the room
it creeps slower than a philosopher,
it makes a bright puddle
that alters like an amoeba,
it climbs the door
as though it were afraid it would fall.

In a few minutes it'll make this page
an assaulting dazzle. I'll pull a curtain
sideways. I'll snip
a few yards off those millions of miles
and, tailor of the universe, sit quietly
stitching my few ragged days together.

Norman MacCaig

Bluetit on a string of peanuts

A cubic inch of some stars
weighs a hundred tons – Blue tit,
who could measure the power
of your tiny spark of energy? Your hair-thin legs
(one north-east, one due west) support
a scrap of volcano, four inches
of hurricane: and, seeing me you make the sound
of a grain of sawdust being sawn
by the minutest of saws.

Norman MacCaig

Rationalists

Rationalists, wearing square hats,
Think, in square rooms,
Looking at the door,
Looking at the ceiling.
They confine themselves
To right-angled triangles.
If they tried rhomboids,
Cones, waving lines, ellipses –
As, for example, the ellipse of the half-moon –
Rationalists would wear sombreros.

Wallace Stevens

The Peace of Wild Things

When despair grows in me
and I wake in the middle of the night at the least sound
in fear of what my life and my children's lives may be,
I go and lie down where the wood drake
rests in his beauty on the water,
and the great heron feeds. I come into the peace of wild things
who do not tax their lives with forethought
of grief. I come into the presence of still water.
And I feel above me the day – blind stars waiting with their light.
For a time
I rest in the grace of the world, and am free.

Wendell Berry

Pax

All that matters is to be at one with the living God
to be a creature in the house of the God of life.

Like a cat asleep on a chair
at peace, in peace
and at one with the master of the house, with the mistress,
at home, at home in the house of the living,
sleeping on the hearth, and yawning before the fire.

Sleeping on the hearth of the living world,
yawning at home before the fire of life
feeling the presence of the living God
like a great reassurance
a deep calm in the heart
a presence
as of a master sitting at the board
in his own and greater being,
in the house of life.

D H Lawrence

And the Days Are Not Full Enough

And the days are not full enough
And the nights are not full enough
And life slips by like a field mouse
          Not shaking the grass

Ezra Pound

God's Grandeur

The world is charged with the grandeur of God.
    It will flame out, like shining from shook foil;
    It gathers to a greatness, like the ooze of oil
Crushed. Why do men then now not reck his rod?
Generations have trod, have trod, have trod;
    And all is seared with trade; bleared, smeared with toil;
    And wears man's smudge and shares man's smell: the soil
Is bare now, nor can foot feel, being shod.

And for all this, nature is never spent;
    There lives the dearest freshness deep down things;
And though the last lights off the black West went
    Oh, morning, at the brown brink eastward, springs –
Because the Holy Ghost over the bent
    World broods with warm breast and with ah! bright wings.

Gerard Manley Hopkins

from *Divina Commedia*

Oft have I seen at some cathedral door
    A labourer, pausing in the dust and heat,
    Lay down his burden, and with reverent feet
    Enter, and cross himself, and on the floor
Kneel to repeat his paternoster o'er;
    Far off the noises of the world retreat;
    The loud vociferations of the street
    Become an undistinguishable roar.
So, as I enter here from day to day,
    And leave my burden at this minster gate,
    Kneeling in prayer, and not ashamed to pray,
The tumult of the time disconsolate
    To inarticulate murmurs dies away,
    While the eternal ages watch and wait.

Henry Wadsworth Longfellow

I saw him standing

Under the dark trees, there he stands,
there he stands; shall he not draw my eyes?
I thought I knew a little
how he compels, beyond all things, but now
he stands there in the shadows. It will be
Oh, such a daybreak, such bright morning,
when I shall wake to see him as he is.

He is called Rose of Sharon, for his skin
is clear, his skin is flushed with blood,
his body lovely and exact; how he compels
beyond ten thousand rivals. There he stands,
my friend, the friend of guilt and helplessness,
To steer my hollow body
over the sea.

The earth is full of masks and fetishes,
what is there here for me? are these like him?
Keep company with him and you will know:
no kin, no likeness to those empty eyes.
He is a stranger to them all, great Jesus.
What is there here for me? I know
what I have longed for. Him to hold
me always.

Translated by Rowan Williams from
Yr Arglwydd Iesu, a poem by **Ann Griffiths**

16

As the Team's Head Brass

As the team's head-brass flashed out on the turn
The lovers disappeared into the wood.
I sat among the boughs of the fallen elm
That strewed the angle of the fallow, and
Watched the plough narrowing a yellow square
Of charlock. Every time the horses turned
Instead of treading me down, the ploughman leaned
Upon the handles to say or ask a word,
About the weather, next about the war.
Scraping the share he faced towards the wood,
And screwed along the furrow till the brass flashed
Once more.
The blizzard felled the elm whose crest
I sat in, by a woodpecker's round hole,
The ploughman said. 'When will they take it away? '
'When the war's over.' So the talk began –
One minute and an interval of ten,
A minute more and the same interval.
'Have you been out? ' 'No.' 'And don't want to, perhaps? '
'If I could only come back again, I should.
I could spare an arm, I shouldn't want to lose
A leg. If I should lose my head, why, so,
I should want nothing more...Have many gone
From here? ' 'Yes.' 'Many lost? ' 'Yes, a good few.
Only two teams work on the farm this year.
One of my mates is dead. The second day
In France they killed him. It was back in March,
The very night of the blizzard, too. Now if
He had stayed here we should have moved the tree.'
'And I should not have sat here. Everything
Would have been different. For it would have been
Another world.' 'Ay, and a better, though
If we could see all all might seem good.' Then
The lovers came out of the wood again:
The horses started and for the last time
I watched the clods crumble and topple over
After the ploughshare and the stumbling team.

Edward Thomas

Prayer

Some days, although we cannot pray, a prayer
utters itself. So, a woman will lift
her head from the sieve of her hands and stare
at the minims sung by a tree, a sudden gift.

Some nights, although we are faithless, the truth
enters our hearts, that small familiar pain;
then a man will stand stock-still, hearing his youth
in the distant Latin chanting of a train.

Pray for us now. Grade I piano scales
console the lodger looking out across
a Midlands town. Then dusk, and someone calls
a child's name as though they named their loss.

Darkness outside. Inside, the radio's prayer –
Rockall. Malin. Dogger. Finisterre.

Carol Ann Duffy

Everyone sang

Everyone suddenly burst out singing;
And I was filled with such delight
As prisoned birds must find in freedom,
Winging wildly across the white
Orchards and dark-green fields; on–on–and out of sight.

Everyone's voice was suddenly lifted;
And beauty came like the setting sun:
My heart was shaken with tears; and horror
Drifted away ... O, but Everyone
Was a bird; and the song was wordless; the singing will never be done.

Siegfried Sassoon

Swineherd

When all this is over, said the swineherd,
I mean to retire, where
Nobody will have heard about my special skills
And conversation is mainly about the weather.

I intend to learn how to make coffee, at least as well
As the Portuguese lay-sister in the kitchen
And polish the brass fenders every day.
I want to lie awake at night
Listening to cream crawling to the top of the jug
And the water lying soft in the cistern.

I want to see an orchard where the trees grow in straight lines
and the yellow fox finds shelter between the navy-blue trunks,
Where it gets dark early in summer
And the apple-blossom is allowed to wither on the bough.

Eiléan ní Chuilleanáin

The Empty Church

They laid this stone trap
for him, enticing him with candles,
as though he would come like some huge moth
out of the darkness to beat there.
Ah, he had burned himself
before in the human flame
and escaped, leaving the reason
torn. He will not come any more

to our lure. Why, then, do I kneel still
striking my prayers on a stone
heart? Is it in hope one
of them will ignite yet and throw
on its illumined walls the shadow
of someone greater than I can understand?

RS Thomas

Song

Only the wanderer
Knows England's graces,
Or can anew see clear
Familiar faces.

And who loves joy as he
That dwells in shadows?
Do not forget me quite,
O Severn meadows.

Ivor Gurney

Strange to think

Strange to think of this private wood
which those around me never enter.
On soft spring days, I pick my way
between clumps of dancing thoughts
growing beneath the strong oaks of real life.
In summer, the delicate tendrils of dreams
wrap their frail fresh stalks
round the stakes and wires I placed
so carefully there in winter.
In the autumn, their flowers
turn to fruit, round and plump –
some to be picked, some discarded,
some left for another day.
High over the wood
my thoughts and passions circle the trees
hop between branches
sing, sometimes, to you who visit.

Alison Morgan

First Thing

The last bit of the dream is letters falling,
soft and regular, the papery flutter
rhythmic on the mat. Not unlike
grey tides licking sand. Waking
is water leaking in; the stuff
out there wobbles and swells
and settles grudgingly into a dryish
daytime shape. And the letters
leaking in resolve themselves
as the dry short breaths
of a nextdoor body, finding
its way out of the night
into slow breakfast time,
the food, the light, a few words,
and the apprehensive, unavoidable
opening of envelopes.

Rowan Williams

The Uninvited Guest

He seems to come in like the leaves -
Blown in at the open window,
And always on a light and airy day.
Never in stormy weather.
And always, I've noticed,
At an inconvenient time -
Right in the middle of the washing.
He looks at me and shows me these holes in his hands.
And, well, I can see them in his feet.
'Not again,' I say.
'Please don't stand there bleeding
All over the kitchen floor.'

Sometimes he comes softly, sadly,
At night - close, by the side of my bed -
Sometimes I latch the door —

But he never goes away.

Thelma Laycock

A Hymn to God the Father

Wilt thou forgive that sin where I begun,
  Which is my sin, though it were done before?
Wilt thou forgive those sins, through which I run,
  And do them still: though still I do deplore?
    When thou hast done, thou hast not done,
      For, I have more.

Wilt thou forgive that sin by which I have won
  Others to sin? and, made my sin their door?
Wilt thou forgive that sin which I did shun
  A year or two: but wallowed in, a score?
    When thou hast done, thou hast not done,
      For, I have more.

I have a sin of fear, that when I have spun
  My last thread, I shall perish on the shore;
  Swear by thyself, that at my death thy Sun
Shall shine as it shines now, and heretofore;
    And, having done that, thou hast done,
      I fear no more.

John Donne

Sometimes

Sometimes the landscape of my soul
seems like this burnt hillside,
the wind rattling orange leaves on black twigs,
the soil full of ash between the stones.
Sometimes the landscape of my soul
seems like this terrible waste of dead trees.

Walking this afternoon among the charred remains
I found a black stump sprouting leaves
and new grass thinly veiling
a delicate oak sapling
in this, the ravaged landscape of my soul.

Susan Fisher

The Spirit must scream
Plummet down
Like a bird of prey
   And sit   fierce
Talons clenched
In your bleeding lips

And your words become
His Word
And his Word become
Your words
That your speech
Dead in the agony of self
Might be resurrected
In self-extinction.

John Leax

Song of Solomon

My beloved spake, and said unto me, Rise up, my love, my fair
        one, and come away.
For, lo, the winter is past, the rain is over, and gone.
The flowers appear on the earth; the time of the singing of
        birds is come, and the voice of the turtle is heard in our land;
The fig tree putteth forth her green figs, and the vines with
        the tender grape give a good smell.
Arise, my love, my fair one, and come away.

King James Bible

Sonnet

Shall I compare thee to a summer's day?
Thou art more lovely and more temperate:
Rough winds do shake the darling buds of May,
And summer's lease hath all too short a date:
Sometime too hot the eye of heaven shines,
And often is his gold complexion dimm'd;
And every fair from fair sometime declines,
By chance or nature's changing course untrimm'd;
But thy eternal summer shall not fade
Nor lose possession of that fair thou owest;
Nor shall Death brag thou wander'st in his shade,
When in eternal lines to time thou growest:
So long as men can breathe or eyes can see,
So long lives this and this gives life to thee.

William Shakespeare

The Trees

The trees are coming into leaf
Like something almost being said;
The recent buds relax and spread,
Their greenness is a kind of grief.

Is it that they are born again
And we grow old? No, they die too.
Their yearly trick of looking new
Is written down in rings of grain.

Yet still the unresting castles thresh
 In fullgrown thickness every May.
Last year is dead, they seem to say,
Begin afresh, afresh, afresh.

Philip Larkin

Delay

The radiance of that star that leans on me
Was shining years ago. The light that now
Glitters up there my eye may never see,
And so the time lag teases me with how

Love that loves now may not reach me until
Its first desire is spent. The star's impulse
Must wait for eyes to claim it beautiful
And love arrived may find us somewhere else.

Elizabeth Jennings

The Pause

Sentences, like people,
need spaces to breathe.
Between the full stop
and the Capital
lies   the pause.

Without the space,
sentences are breathless;
without the Sabbath,
life is restless;
without the pause,
the rest is lifeless.

Sentences, like God,
have a preferential option
for   the pause.

Graham Kings

There is a tide in the affairs of men
Which, taken at the flood, leads on to fortune;
Omitted, all the voyage of their life
Is bound in shallows and in miseries.
On such a full sea are we now afloat,
And we must take the current when it serves,
Or lose our ventures.

William Shakespeare (Julius Caesar, IV.ii.269–276)

The argument of his book

I sing of brooks, of blossoms, birds, and bowers,
Of April, May, of June, and July-flowers;
I sing of May-poles, hock-carts, wassails, wakes,
Of bridegrooms, brides and of their bridal-cakes;
I write of youth, of love, and have access
By these to sing of cleanly wantonness;
I sing of dews, of rains, and piece by piece
Of balm, of oil, of spice and ambergris;
I sing of times trans-shifting, and I write
How roses first came red and lilies white;
I write of groves, of twilights, and I sing
The court of Mab, and of the fairy king;
I write of Hell; I sing (and ever shall)
Of Heaven, and hope to have it after all.

Robert Herrick

A humble request

All right
I understand
I can't come in.
My life was –
I know.
But
if I could just
sit outside the gates
for a few minutes
and listen to the music?

Michael Swan

A Quiet Roar

one

he lays his left hand along the beam
hand that moulded clay into fluttering birds
hand that cupped wild flowers to learn their peace
hand that stroked the bee's soft back and touched death's sting

two

he stretches his right hand across the grain
hand that blessed a dead corpse quick
hand that smeared blind spittle into sight
hand that burgeoned bread, smoothed down the rumpled sea

three

he stands laborious
sagging, split,
homo erectus, poor bare forked thing
hung on nails like a picture

he is not beautiful
blood sweats from him in rain

far off where we are lost, desert dry
thunder begins its quiet roar
the first drops startle us alive
the cloud no bigger
than a man's hand

Veronica Zundel

Painting from 'Stages of the Cross' by Peter Clare

I will live

I will live and survive and be asked
How they slammed my head against a trestle
How I had to freeze at nights
How my hair started to turn grey
But I'll smile. And will crack some joke
And brush away the encroaching shadow
And will render homage to the dry September
That became my second birth.
And I'll be asked, "Doesn't it hurt you to remember?"
Not being deceived by my outward flippancy
But the former names will detonate my memory –
Magnificent as old cannon.
And I will tell of the best people in all the earth,
The most tender, but also the most invincible.
How they said farewell, how they went to be tortured,
How they waited for letters from their loved ones.
And I'll be asked : what helped us to live
When there were neither letters, nor any news – only walls,
And the cold of the cell, and the blather of official lies,
And the sickening promises made in exchange for betrayal.
And I will tell of the first beauty I saw in captivity.
A frost-covered window! No spyholes, nor walls,
Nor cell-bars, nor the long-endured pain –
Only a blue radiance on a tiny pane of glass –
A cast pattern – none more beautiful could be dreamt!
The more clearly you looked, the more powerfully blossomed
Those brigand forests, campfires and birds!
And how many times there was bitter cold weather
And how many windows sparkled after that one –
But never was it repeated
That upheaval of rainbow ice!
And anyway, what good would it be to me now,
And what would be the pretext for that festival?
Such a gift can only be received once
And perhaps is only needed once.

Irina Ratushinskaya

Cracks

There are cracks in my world.
I noticed them one day and now they are everywhere:
Sinister hairline cracks that start and finish out of sight,
cracks that grow and gape and laugh at my certainties.
My world has been declared unsafe.

I have tried to paper them over,
paint them out,
move the furniture to hide them,
but they always return,
cracks that hang like question marks in my mind

And now I begin to think:
Why do the cracks appear?
From where do they come?
They have made my room unsafe
BUT

They have thrown it open to new horizons,
drawn back curtains,
raised long-closed shutters.
One day I looked and a crack had become a window.
Step through, it said, what have you to fear?
Do you wish to stay in your crumbling room?

And then I remembered a childhood dream,
watching the egg of some exotic bird,
oval and perfect, spotted blue and cream.
I wished to hold that egg and keep it on a shelf
BUT

As I watched it cracks appeared.
Tiny fissures spread like zigzag ripples.
It broke in two and life struggled to its feet,
wet and weak and blinking at the world.
 Without those cracks that egg could hold
no more than rotting stagnant death.

Without its cracks my world would be
a room without a view.
Cracks may be uncomfortable disturbing gaps
BUT

Could it be I need them?
Do you believe in cracks?
Because I keep looking for God in the room
and find he is hiding in the cracks

Dave Bookless

Windharp

The sounds of Ireland,
that restless whispering
you never get away
from, seeping out of
low bushes and grass,
heatherbells and fern,
wrinkling bog pools,
scraping tree branches,
light hunting cloud,
sound hounding sight,
a hand ceaselessly
combing and stroking
the landscape, till
the valley gleams
like the pile upon
a mountain pony's coat.

John Montague

Easter

Nation after nation came
One by one, up the path,
Past the mailbox
And the picket fence, past the petunias,
Past the sign "Beware of Dog,"
Past the bulldog sleeping
With a smile on his face.
Each one came in turn
And stood on the welcome mat

And pounded in a nail, one at a time.
One through the foot, one through
The hand. A big shot from New York
Came and smacked one
Through the kidney. The kids came up
With sticky hands and took
Their licks. Bam. "Junior's got
Good hands,
Marge, don't you think?"
Marge was busy pounding.
She bent the nail.
The policeman came up.

"Just one, lady. Get along."
He went away, up
and down the long line
That stretched for centuries.
"Don't push. You there, come with me."
Etcetera.
Until only the sweeper was left.
Until what had been
A spread-eagled body
Lying whiter than a wedding invitation
Looked more like some kind of
Crazy iron armadillo,
There were so many nails.

Dark came and the winds came trampling
Out of the east
Like bulls. The moon looked
The other way. But then it grew,
Like an idea, huge and red,
Wavy with heat.
Everything panicked. Trees shrieked
And withered in the moon's heat.
Birds rose like helium balloons.
Telephone poles popped like corks.
The night was brighter than
A hamburg stand.
The night was hotter than
A hamburg stand.

At last
There came a popping sound
And nails were popping off
The crazy iron armadillo
Like buttons. All the nails.
Fizzing high into the air
Like Roman candles,
Until the spread-eagled body
Once again lay white,
Rising like bread.
And the world
and all the wrappers
Peeled away.

Randall J VanderMey

My Fiftieth year...

My fiftieth year had come and gone,
And I sat, a solitary man,
In a crowded London shop,
An open book and empty cup
On the marble table-top.

While on the shop and street I gazed
My body of a sudden blazed;
And twenty minutes more or less
It seemed, so great my happiness,
that I was blessèd and could bless.

W B Yeats

Sometimes

Sometimes things don't go, after all,
from bad to worse. Some years, muscadel
faces down frost; green thrives; the crops don't fail,
Sometimes a man aims high, and all goes well.

A people sometimes will step back from war,
elect an honest man, decide they care
enough, that they can't leave some stranger poor.
Some men become what they were born for.

Sometimes our best efforts do not go
amiss; sometimes we do as we meant to.
The sun will sometimes melt a field of sorrow
that seemed hard frozen; may it happen for you.

Anon

The Sunflower - *After Eugenio Montale*

Bring me the sunflower so that I may plant it in my field
whose earth, exposed to winds from off the sea, is scorched and dry;
then all day long its troubled upturned face will be revealed,
sending a yellow signal to the blue reflecting sky.
Dark things seek their opposite — the clarity of day;
and bodies spend their substance in the urgent flux and flow
of colours, just as colours do in strains of music; so
it is the destiny of destinies to pass away.
Bring me the plant, my love, that leads the traveller to a place
where blond transparencies are formed and, as they form, take flight
and life unmakes itself, from solid essence into hazy space;
bring me the sunflower driven to insanity by light.

John Richmond

Portami il girasole

Portami il girasole ch'io lo trapianti
nel mio terreno bruciato dal salino,
e mostri tutto il giorno agli azzurri specchianti
del cielo l'ansietà del suo volto giallino.
Tendono alla chiarità le cose oscure,
si esauriscono i corpi in un fluire
di tinte: queste in musiche. Svanire
è dunque la ventura delle venture.
Portami tu la pianta che conduce
dove sorgono bionde trasparenze
e vapora la vita quale essenza;
portami il girasole impazzito di luce.

Eugenio Montale

The Bright Field

I have seen the sun break through
to illuminate a small field
for a while, and gone my way
and forgotten it. But that was the pearl
of great price, the one field that had
the treasure in it. I realize now
that I must give all that I have
to possess it. Life is not hurrying

on to a receding future, nor hankering after
an imagined past. It is the turning
aside like Moses to the miracle
of the lit bush, to a brightness
that seemed as transitory as your youth
 once, but is the eternity that awaits you.

RS Thomas

Happiness

A state you must dare not enter
   with hopes of staying,
quicksand in the marshes, and all

the roads leading to a castle
   that doesn't exist.
But there it is, as promised,

with its perfect bridge above
   the crocodiles,
and its doors forever open.

Stephen Dunn

Standing upon Westminster Bridge

Earth has not anything to show more fair:
Dull would he be of soul who could pass by
A sight so touching in its majesty:
This City now doth, like a garment, wear
The beauty of the morning; silent, bare,
Ships, towers, domes, theatres, and temples lie
Open unto the fields, and to the sky;
All bright and glittering in the smokeless air.
Never did sun more beautifully steep
In his first splendour, valley, rock, or hill;
Ne'er saw I, never felt, a calm so deep!
The river glideth at his own sweet will:
Dear God! the very houses seem asleep;
And all that mighty heart is lying still!

William Wordsworth

Westminster Bridge in 1828

Leisure

What is the life if, full of care,
We have no time to stand and stare?

No time to stand beneath the boughs
And stare as long as sheep or cows.

No time to see, when woods we pass,
Where squirrels hide their nuts in grass.

No time to see, in broad daylight,
Streams full of stars, like skies at night.

No time to turn at Beauty's glance,
And watch her feet, how they can dance.

No time to wait till her mouth can
Enrich that smile her eyes began.

A poor life this, if full of care,
We have no time to stand and stare.

W H Davies

Black Rook in Rainy Weather

On the stiff twig up there
Hunches a wet black rook
Arranging and rearranging its feathers in the rain.
I do not expect a miracle
Or an accident

To set the sight on fire
In my eye, nor seek
Any more in the desultory weather some design,
But let spotted leaves fall as they fall,
Without ceremony, or portent.

Although, I admit, I desire,
Occasionally, some backtalk
From the mute sky, I can't honestly complain:
A certain minor light may still
Lean incandescent

Out of kitchen table or chair
As if a celestial burning took
Possession of the most obtuse objects now and then --
Thus hallowing an interval
Otherwise inconsequent

By bestowing largesse, honour,
One might say love. At any rate, I now walk
Wary (for it could happen
Even in this dull, ruinous landscape); skeptical,
Yet politic; ignorant

Of whatever angel may choose to flare
Suddenly at my elbow. I only know that a rook
Ordering its black feathers can so shine
As to seize my senses, haul
My eyelids up, and grant

A brief respite from fear

Of total neutrality. With luck,
Trekking stubborn through this season
Of fatigue, I shall
Patch together a content

Of sorts. Miracles occur,
If you care to call those spasmodic
Tricks of radiance miracles. The wait's begun again,
The long wait for the angel,
For that rare, random descent.

Sylvia Plath

The Coming

And God held in his hand
A small globe. Look, he said.
The son looked. Far off
As through water, he saw
A scorched land of fierce
Colour. The light burned
There; crusted buildings
Cast their shadows: a bright
Serpent, a river
Uncoiled itself, radiant
With slime.
                    On a bare
Hill a bare tree saddened
The sky. Many people
Held out their thin arms
To it, as though waiting
For a vanished April
to return to its crossed
Boughs. The son watched
Them. Let me go there, he said.

R S Thomas

The Golden Road to Samarkand

THE CHIEF MERCHANT:
> We gnaw the nail of hurry. Master, away!

ONE OF THE WOMEN:
> O turn your eyes to where your children stand. Is not Bagdad the
> beautiful? 0, stay!

THE MERCHANTS (*in chorus*):
> We take the Golden Road to Samarkand.

HASSAN:
> Sweet to ride forth at evening from the wells,
> When shadows pass gigantic on the sand,
> And softly through the silence beat the bells
> Along the Golden Road to Samarkand.

ISHAK:
> We travel not for trafficking alone;
> By hotter winds our fiery hearts are fanned:
> For lust of knowing what should not be known,
> We take the Golden Road to Samarkand.

THE MASTER OF THE CARAVAN:
> Open the gate, 0 watchman of the night!

THE WATCHMAN:
> Ho, travellers, I open. For what land
> Leave you the dim-moon city of delight?

THE MERCHANTS (*with a shout*):
> We take the Golden Road to Samarkand! The Caravan passes
> through the gate.

THE WATCHMAN (*consoling the women*):
> What would ye, ladies? It was ever thus. Men are unwise and
> curiously planned.

A WOMAN:
> They have their dreams, and do not think of us.
> *The* WATCHMAN *closes the gate*.

VOICES OF THE CARAVAN (*in the distance singing*):
> We take the Golden Road to Samarkand.

James Elroy Flecker

These are the closing lines from *Hassan*, a play first performed in 1923.
The play traces the preparations for the great journey of the camel
caravan of merchants and pilgrims to Samarkand. The golden gate of
Samarkand becomes a symbol of human yearning.

Sergeant Brown's parrot

Many policemen wear upon their shoulders
Cunning little radios. To pass away the time
They talk about the traffic to them, listen to the news,
And it helps them to Keep Down Crime.

But Sergeant Brown, he wears upon his shoulder
A tall green parrot as he's walking up and down
And all the parrot says is "Who's-a-pretty-boy-then?"
"I am," says Sergeant Brown.

Kit Wright

Journey

In a village by the sea, with painted beach huts
I stood and waited, not knowing who would come, or why.
The village was my childhood, and the sun rose high
over the marshes. Harriers hunted, a bittern boomed,
fishing nets and glass floats decked the church
where the future unfurled its misty wings.
I left the sea behind and travelled overland;
libraries bestowed degrees, and marriage children
the passing of the years, maturity
but as I return to walk along the pebbled shore
a carnelian glows amongst the other stones
never previously noticed, but gathered now as mine.
The sea ebbs and flows, unfolds my life's design.

Alison Morgan

White for Harvest

The harvest has been taken, beautifully and on time
On a glorious August day.
Your Combine swirled the cloying dust around –
But, there, the deed was done:
The showing in the barren of the field.

Yesterday you returned and patiently harrowed the remains;
Looking forward, touching the new cycle.
And now, as I sit here quietly in the early morning,
The crows track the furrows, gleaning the insects
Who have lost their roof,
Whose world has been opened to the sky.

This is a time of plenty,
But also one of loss and change.
Where gentle ranks of nodding ears stood waiting,
Patient in their goldening,
There now grow only the remains
Stretching out into the mists of mornings undiscovered;
Stalked solemnly by black birds with ageless resignation,
Like ushers at an unexpected feast.

Martin Cavender

The Dove

I wanted the dove for a long time but had no money to buy it
only cash that had to be kept just then for houses and eating
and children and I had enough beautiful things, but I
wanted the dove and just before Christmas last
year I fell and I carried it home. Now, never
wrapped or tinselled, it broods in this still
white room, crackle-glazed, shiny, with
sharp round eyes, the colour of
creamed yeast. it's warm to
my touch not having the
chill of a dead thing
stark under matted feathers
and its eyes are bright, not the
rinsed black holes of those magotty
lumps that we bury if children are watching
or furtively kick under trees, it's a good symbol
of holiness having been neither alive nor dead. Here, in this
slow half light, waiting for me every sunrise this dove
might always have been
here a tender
I AM

Ann Pilling

Ode

We are the music-makers,
And we are the dreamers of dreams,
Wandering by lone sea-breakers,
And sitting by desolate streams;
World-losers and world-forsakers,
On whom the pale moon gleams:
Yet we are the movers and shakers
Of the world for ever, it seems

With wonderful deathless ditties
We build up the world's great cities.
And out of a fabulous story
We fashion art empire's glory:
One man with a dream, at pleasure,
Shall go forth and conquer a crown;
And three with a new song's measure
Can trample an empire down.

We, in the ages lying
In the buried past of the earth.
Built Nineveh with our sighing,
And Babel itself with our mirth;
And o'erthrew them with prophesying
To the old of the new world's worth;
For each age is a dream that is dying,
Or one that is coming to birth.

Arthur O'Shaughnessy

47

High Flight

Oh! I have slipped the surly bonds of earth,
And danced the skies on laughter-silvered wings;
Sunward I've climbed, and joined the tumbling mirth
Of sun-split clouds, – and done a hundred things
You have not dreamed of – wheeled and soared and swung
High in the sunlit silence. Hov'ring there
I've chased the shouting wind along, and flung
My eager craft through footless halls of air...
Up, up the long, delirious, burning blue
I've topped the wind-swept heights with easy grace
Where never lark or even eagle flew –
And, while with silent lifting mind I've trod
The high untrespassed sanctity of space,
Put out my hand, and touched the face of God.

John Gillespie Magee

RCAF Supermarine Spitfire

Growing, Flying, Happening

Say the soft bird's name, but do not be surprised to see it fall
headlong, struck skyless, into its pigeonhole –
columba palumbus and you have it dead,
wedged, neat, unwinged in your head.

That the black-backed tatter-winged thing
straking the harbour water and then plummeting
down, to come up, sleek head a-cock,
a minted herring shining in its beak,
is a *guillemot*, is neither here nor there
in the amazement of its rising,
wings slicing the stiff salt air.

That of that spindling spear-leaved plant,
wearing the palest purple umbel,
many-headed, blue-tinted, stilt-stalked
at the stream-edge, one should say briefly
angelica, is by-the-way (though grant
the name itself to be beautiful).
Grant too that any name
makes its own music, that *bryony, sally-my-handsome*
burst at their sound into flower,
and that *falcon* and *phalarope* fly off in the ear,
still,
names are for saying at home.

The point is the seeing – the grace
beyond recognition, the ways
of the bird rising, unnamed, unknown,
beyond the range of language, beyond its noun.
Eyes open on growing, flying, happening,
and go on opening. Manifold, the world
dawns on unrecognizing, realising eyes.
Amazement is the thing.
Not love, but the astonishment of loving.

Alastair Reid

The Catch

Forget
the long, smouldering
afternoon. It is

this moment
when the ball scoots
off the edge

of the bat; upwards,
backwards, falling
seemingly

beyond him
yet he reaches
and picks it

out
of its loop
like

an apple
from a branch,
the first of the season.

Simon Armitage

Indifference

When Jesus came to Birmingham
they simply passed him by.
They never hurt a hair of him
they simply let him die.
For men had grown more tender
and they would not give him pain.
They only just passed down the street
and left him in the rain.

Still Jesus cried, 'Forgive them, for they
know not what they do.'
And still it rained the wintry rain
that drenched him through and through.

The crowds went home and left the streets
without a soul to see.
And Jesus crouched against a wall
and cried for Calvary.

G A Studdert Kennedy

The Leader

I wanna be the leader
I wanna be the leader
Can I be the leader?
Can I? Can I?
Promise? Promise?
Yippee, I'm the leader
I'm the leader

OK what shall we do?

Roger McGough

Guests

Oh, the trouble we've had
with this building over the years!
Heavens, the unwanted guests!

Rats, do you remember,
after the Dustbin Men's strike,
getting, somehow, into the wafers?
And trying to get the Council round
before Harvest Festival
to flush them out?

And then pigeons constantly
blocking up the drains
with those stupid bunches of twigs
they call nests.

And then for years, and years and years,
Death-Watch
(for those of us who can still hear)
Tap-tap-tapping in quiet bits of the service ...
Lord! When the man told us
what it would cost to sort that out
well, it nearly broke our spirit
but we managed.
We managed.

And squirrels in the roof
several years running.
They had to be gassed, eventually.
Yes, it's certainly been a labour of love.

And now, I hate to say it but:
We, The Committee,
are pretty sure someone has been
SLEEPING IN THE CHURCH.
I can't imagine where they're getting in.
But they'll have to go.
Absolutely the last straw.

As I remind my committee,
when you take on a building of this size,
you take on a huge responsibility.

Lucy Berry

Conversion

He was a born loser,
accident-prone too;
never won a lottery,
married a girl who
couldn't cook, broke
his leg the day before
the wedding
and forgot the ring.
He was the kind
who ended up behind a post
in almost any
auditorium. Planes
he was booked to fly on
were delayed
by engine trouble
with sickening regularity.
His holidays at the beach
were almost always
ruined by rain. All
his apples turned out
wormy. His letters
came back marked
'Moved, left no
address.' And it was
his car that was cited
for speeding
from among a flock of others
going 60 in a
55 mile zone.

So it was a real shocker
when he found himself
elected, chosen by Grace
for Salvation, felt
the exhilaration of
an undeserved and wholly
unexpected joy

and tasted, for the
first time, the Glory
of being on
the winning side.

Luci Shaw

If People Disapprove of You

Make being disapproved of your hobby.
Make being disapproved of your aim.
Devise new ways of scoring points
In the Being Disapproved Of Game.

Let them disapprove in their dozens.
Let them disapprove in their hordes.
You'll find that being disapproved of
Builds character, brings rewards

Just like any form of striving.
Don't be arrogant; don't coast
On your high disapproval rating.
Try to be disapproved of most.

At this point, if it's useful,
Draw a pie-chart or a graph.
Show it to someone who disapproves.
When they disapprove, just laugh.

Count the emotions you provoke:
Anger, suspicion, shock.
One point for each of these and two
For every boat you rock.

Feel yourself warming to your task –
You do it bloody well.
At last you've found an area
In which you can excel.

Savour the thrill of risk without
The fear of getting caught.
Whether they sulk or scream or pout,
Enjoy your new-found sport.

Meanwhile all those who disapprove
While you are having fun
Won't even know your game exists
So tell yourself you've won.

Sophie Hannah

Rembrandt's Sandwich

An artist sits in a café, watching a man.
Her eyes are drawn to the warming red of his coat,
the grateful way he cups his steaming drink,
 worries at a sandwich; rabbi, mumbling prayer.

The artist watches, and begins to see.
The man is facing the past, in its winter light.
He could be someone known, or wearing a mask.
He is also watching: menu readers, shoppers,
prodigal children, loose, daughters and sons.

The artist begins to catch him in her pocket book;
the angle of his mind, worn by remembering,
 halter of his shoulders, phrasing of bearded jaw
as if rehearsing a speech he'd half-forgotten,
small hopes in half-closed eyes, small hopes, returning.
The artist jots notes: scarlets, pleats on rags.

She pauses, leaves a gap in front of the man,
a space for a tumbled body and bronzed, shaved head
re-casting Rembrandt: who painted a father who watched
roads and crowds for so long, till holes in his hands
were re-filled by his son's return. Servants in shadow
wondering if it was better to smile, or marvel.
Similar beginning? Perhaps Rembrandt, over a loaf,
saw such a drape of red, same wondering eyes,
watched a man wait for news, suspended judgement,
recalled a story, set his bread aside. Drew.

Martyn Halsall

Slave

'The sculpture is already complete within the marble block, before I start my work. It is already there, I just have to chisel away the superfluous material.' – Michelangelo

Once, when you were trapped,
there was only one man to see you, and he stroked
your stone with his chisel, set
to with his excavations and let
you out.

This angel tapped at
your heart and told you he knew
who you were, gave you a name
– breathed life into your veins –
and carved your sinewed muscle,
born fighting and you struggled to be free
and he with his mighty sculptor's hands
played God, and made you with a heart
of stone, with a mind of marble.

Now as I stand at your proud feet
my pale eyes wonder
who was the greater:
the giant borne of everlasting rock
or his fleeting, skilful maker?

Katy Morgan

from **Prayer**

A kind of tune, which all things hear and fear;
Softness, and peace, and joy, and love, and bliss,
  Exalted manna, gladness of the best,
  Heaven in ordinary, man well dressed,
The milky way, the bird of Paradise,
  Church-bells beyond the stars heard, the soul's blood,
  The land of spices; something understood.

George Herbert

Linen sheets at the car boot sale, France

It's heavy to the touch,
Gracious as it falls through my hands;
Small, soft hands, not used to weight.
But the weight of this is delicious,
Courteous, folding, flowing
As it wraps itself around my fingers.

Embracing, kind, lingering on the surface,
Not sensuous
Cream, with a hint of grey
Every fibre different,
Laid together like nature's collage
Perfectly formed
In ranks and twists and lines
Giving one another
A whisper of room.

Cesca Cavender

Child waking

The child sleeps in the daytime,
With his abandoned, with his jetsam look,
On the bare mattress, across the cot's corner;
Covers and toys thrown out, a routine labour.

Relaxed in sleep and light,
Face upwards, never so clear a prey to eyes;
Like a walled town surprised out of the air –
All life called in, yet all laid bare

To the enemy above –
He has taken cover in daylight, gone to ground
In his own short length, his body strong in bleached
Blue cotton and his arms outstretched.

Now he opens eyes but not
To see at first; they reflect the light like snow,
And I wait in doubt if he sleeps or wakes, till I see
Slight pain of effort at the boundary

And hear how the trifling wound
Of bewilderment fetches a caverned cry
As he crosses out of sleep – at once to recover
His place and poise, and smile as I lift him over.

But I recall the blue –
White snowfield of his eyes empty of sight
High between dream and day, and think how there
The soul might rise visible as a flower.

E J Scovell

58

The Beautiful Lie

He was about four, I think... it was so long ago.
In a garden; he'd done some damage
behind a bright screen of sweet-peas
- snapped a stalk, a stake, I don't recall,
but the grandmother came and saw, and asked him
"Did you do that?"

Now, if she'd said *why* did you do that,
he'd never have denied it. She showed him
he had a choice. I could see in his face
the new sense, the possible. That word and deed
need not match, that you could say the world
different, to suit you.

When he said "No", I swear it was as moving
as the first time a baby's fist clenches
on a finger, as momentous as the first
taste of fruit. I could feel his eyes looking
through a new window, at a world whose form
and colour weren't fixed

but fluid, that poured like a snake, trembled
around the edges like northern lights, shape-shifted
at the spell of a voice. I could sense him filling
like a glass, hear the unreal sea in his ears.
This is how to make songs, create men, paint pictures, tell a story.

I think I made up the screen of sweet-peas.
Maybe they were beans, maybe there was no screen:
it just felt as if there should be, somehow.
And he was my - no, I don't need to tell that.
I know I made up the screen. And I recall very well
what he had done

Sheenagh Pugh

You,

> with your blonde hair and big eyes,
bare feet and those little rolls of fat
in the places where you bend,
what might you become?

You haven't met French yet, never
read a poem, never been all the way down
to the bottom of the garden;
you haven't a scar like a little sickle
on your right shin, or hair that curls.
Never sat an exam.
Never swum in the sea.

Is it possible, then, that you might become me?

Katy Morgan

Walking away

It is eighteen years ago, almost to the day –
A sunny day with leaves just turning,
The touch-lines new-ruled – since I watched you play
Your first game of football, then, like a satellite
Wrenched from its orbit, go drifting away

Behind a scatter of boys. I can see
You walking away from me towards the school
With the pathos of a half-fledged thing set free
Into a wilderness, the gait of one
Who finds no path where the path should be.

That hesitant figure, eddying away
Like a winged seed loosened from its parent stem,
Has something I never quite grasp to convey
About nature's give-and-take – the small, the scorching
Ordeals which fire one's irresolute clay.

I have had worse partings, but none that so
Gnaws at my mind still. Perhaps it is roughly
Saying what God alone could perfectly show –
How selfhood begins with a walking away,
And love is proved in the letting go.

Cecil Day Lewis

The sea and the bells

I came here to count the bells
which live in the sea,
ring in the sea,
beneath the sea.

That's why I came here.

Pablo Neruda

Sea Longing

A thousand miles beyond this sun-steeped wall
Somewhere the waves creep cool along the sand,
The ebbing tide forsakes the listless land
With the old murmur, long and musical;
The windy waves mount up and curve and fall,
And round the rocks the foam blows up like snow -
Tho' I am inland far, I hear and know,
For I was born the sea's eternal thrall.
I would that I were there and over me
The cold insistence of the tide would roll,
Quenching this burning thing men call the soul, -
Then with the ebbing I should drift and be
Less than the smallest shell along the shoal,
Less than the seagulls calling to the sea.

Sara Teasdale

Haiku

Same recognition:
pause, composition, focus:
photo as prayer.

Martyn Halsall

Talking

I wanted so much to tell you everything –
and yet I didn't want to cause you pain.
Wanted so much just to talk and talk –
and then found myself diverted,
or laughing awkwardly, or loud.

How strange. As if the passage
of so many years
had caused a fracture in the flow
of impartation,
a stop within the tender of ideas.

Martin Cavender

Hope

Hope is the thing with feathers
That perches in the soul,
And sings the tune – without the words,
And never stops at all,

And sweetest in the gale is heard;
And sore must be the storm
That could abash the little bird
That kept so many warm.

I've heard it in the chillest land,
And on the strangest sea;
Yet, never, in extremity,
It asked a crumb of me.

Emily Dickinson

Spire

Start with mud. Move it,
excavate with any tools you have,
trowel, spade, hands, fingernails.
Then find stone, dynamite it
out of the quarry, hack or chisel
patiently. Pull it all
on carts and creaking wheels,
drag it down dirt tracks and trails
or haul it on trucks
over miles of highway.

Axe on wood, hammer, nails,
the measured thud of taking,
working, making.
This is how, in a minute calculation
of inches and angles, you let the spire
break through to upper air.
This is how you teach stone to lift
its head to the sky.
This is how, out of clumsy earth,
with daily labour, you set free whatever
it is that you call god.

This is how you draw your human breath
in one pure line across an empty page.

Imtiaz Dharker

Two Bridges

Two bridges, you said, there are two.
Just there, on the water.
And I love it that it's true.
Two bridges dressed in white, waiting for
The reason for their existence
To pass through them, into another country.

Two bridges that are one. Two sentinels.
Two tents of steel. I didn't believe you;
But there suddenly and so clear they were,
Above the brown meanderings and
The distant dangers of the humped
                    and flooding tide.

Martin Cavender

Acquainted with the night

I have been one acquainted with the night.
I have walked out in rain – and back in rain.
I have outwalked the furthest city light.

I have looked down the saddest city lane.
I have passed by the watchman on his beat
And dropped my eyes, unwilling to explain.

I have stood still and stopped the sound of feet
When far away an interrupted cry
Came over houses from another street,

But not to call me back or say good-bye;
And further still at an unearthly height,
A luminary clock against the sky

Proclaimed the time was neither wrong nor right.
I have been one acquainted with the night.

Robert Frost

Lessons of the War : I. Naming of Parts

To-day we have naming of parts. Yesterday,
We had daily cleaning. And to-morrow morning,
We shall have what to do after firing. But to-day,
To-day we have naming of parts. Japonica
Glistens like coral in all of the neighbouring gardens,
    And to-day we have naming of parts.

This is the lower sling swivel. And this
Is the upper sling swivel, whose use you will see,
When you are given your slings. And this is the piling swivel,
Which in your case you have not got. The branches
Hold in the gardens their silent, eloquent gestures,
    Which in our case we have not got.

This is the safety-catch, which is always released
With an easy flick of the thumb. And please do not let me
See anyone using his finger. You can do it quite easy
If you have any strength in your thumb. The blossoms
Are fragile and motionless, never letting anyone see
    Any of them using their finger.

And this you can see is the bolt. The purpose of this
Is to open the breech, as you see. We can slide it
Rapidly backwards and forwards: we call this
Easing the spring. And rapidly backwards and forwards
The early bees are assaulting and fumbling the flowers:
    They call it easing the Spring.

They call it easing the Spring: it is perfectly easy
If you have any strength in your thumb: like the bolt,
And the breech, and the cocking-piece, and the point of balance,
Which in our case we have not got; and the almond-blossom
Silent in all of the gardens and the bees going backwards and forwards,
    For to-day we have naming of parts.

Henry Reed

April Rise

If ever I saw blessing in the air
   I see it now in this still early day
Where lemon-green the vaporous morning drips
   Wet sunlight on the powder of my eye.

Blown bubble-film of blue, the sky wraps round
   Weeds of warm light whose every root and rod
Splutters with soapy green, and all the world
   Sweats with the bead of summer in its bud.

If ever I heard blessing it is there
   Where birds in trees that shoals and shadows are
Splash with their hidden wings and drops of sound
   Break on my ears their crests of throbbing air.

Pure in the haze the emerald sun dilates,
   The lips of sparrows milk the mossy stones,
While white as water by the lake a girl
   Swims her green hand among the gathered swans.

Now, as the almond burns its smoking wick,
   Dropping small flames to light the candled grass;
Now, as my low blood scales its second chance,
   If ever world were blessed, now it is.

Laurie Lee

The Darkling Thrush

I leant upon a coppice gate
   When Frost was spectre-gray,
And Winter's dregs made desolate
   The weakening eye of day.
The tangled vine-stems scored the sky
   Like strings of broken lyres,
And all mankind that haunted nigh
   Had sought their household fires.

The land's sharp features seemed to be
   The Century's corpse outleant,
His crypt the cloudy canopy,
   The wind his death-lament.
The ancient pulse of germ and birth
   Was shrunken hard and dry,
And every spirit upon earth
   Seemed fervourless as I.

At once a voice arose among
   The bleak twigs overhead
In a full-hearted evensong
   Of joy illimited;
An aged thrush, frail, gaunt, and small,
   In blast-beruffled plume,
Had chosen thus to fling his soul
   Upon the growing gloom.

So little cause for carolings
   Of such ecstatic sound
Was written on terrestrial things
   Afar or nigh around,
That I could think there trembled through
   His happy good-night air
Some blessed Hope, whereof he knew
   And I was unaware.

Thomas Hardy

Disclosure

Prayer is like watching for the
Kingfisher. All you can do is
Be where he is likely to appear, and
Wait.
Often, nothing much happens;
There is space, silence and
Expectancy.
No visible sign, only the
Knowledge that he's been there,
And may come again.
Seeing or not seeing cease to matter,
You have been prepared.
But sometimes, when you've almost
Stopped expecting it,
A flash of brightness
Gives encouragement.

Ann Lewin

Yellowhammer

You're a child's bird really, standing
Bright yellow, cheerful, uncomplicated
Perched like a painted knob on the green gorse trees
At nursery teatime, demanding
A little bit of bread and no cheese.

Alison Morgan

On first looking into Chapman's Homer

Much have I travell'd in the realms of gold,
And many goodly states and kingdoms seen;
Round many western islands have I been
Which bards in fealty to Apollo hold.
Oft of one wide expanse had I been told
That deep-brow'd Homer ruled as his demesne:
Yet did I never breathe its pure serene
Till I heard Chapman speak out loud and bold:
Then felt I like some watcher of the skies
When a new planet swims into his ken;
Or like stout Cortez, when with eagle eyes
He stared at the Pacific—and all his men
Look'd at each other with a wild surmise—
Silent, upon a peak in Darien.

John Keats

Monument to the
Discoveries, Lisbon

Buzzard and Alder

Buzzard that folds itself into and becomes nude
alder; alder that insensibly becomes bird –
one life inside the dazzling tree. Together
they do change everything, and forever.

You think, because no news is said here,
not. But rain's rained weather to a rare
blue, so you can see the thinness of it,
I mean the layer they live in, flying in it,

breaking through it minute by glass minute.
Buzzard, hunched in disuse before it
shatters winter, wheeling after food.
Alder, silently glazing us, the dead.

Anne Stevenson

Ode to the Upright Uptight

Ode to the Upright Uptight of a Scottish Church Society
On Politely Discussing Liberation Theology
at One of the Best Hotels in the Land
and Placing me Effectively
on Trial for
Heresy

If
we are
not very careful
the doors of Heaven
will open wide and we
shall all be engulfed... AND
THERE SHALL BE NO DAMNED

Alastair McIntosh

Earth Dweller

It was all the clods at once become
precious; it was the barn, and the shed,
and the windmill, my hands, the crack
Arlie made in the ax handle: oh, let me stay
here humbly, forgotten, to rejoice in it all;
let the sun casually rise and set.
If I have not found the right place,
teach me; for somewhere inside, the clods are
vaulted mansions, lines through the barn sing
for the saints forever, the shed and windmill
rear so glorious the sun shudders like a gong.

Now I know why people worship, carry around
magic emblems, wake up talking dreams
they teach to their children: the world speaks.
The world speaks everything to us.
It is our only friend.

William Stafford

Nothing that happens can hurt me
whether I lose or win;
though life may be changed on the surface
I do my main living within.

Anon

Passion

Full of desire I lay, the sky wounding me,
each cloud a ship without me sailing, each tree
possessing what my soul lacked, tranquillity.

Waiting for the longed-for voice to speak
through the mute telephone, my body grew weak
with the well-known and mortal death, heartbreak.

The language I knew best, my human speech
forsook my fingers, and out of reach
were Homer's ghosts, the savage conches of the beach.

Then the sky spoke to me in language clear,
familiar as the heart, than love more near.
The sky said to my soul, 'You have what you desire!

'Know now that you are born along with these
clouds, winds, and stars, and ever-moving seas
and forest dwellers. This your nature is.

Lift up your heart again without fear,
sleep in the tomb, or breathe the living air,
this world you with the flower and with the tiger share.'

Then I saw every visible substance turn
into immortal, every cell new born
burned with the holy fire of passion.

This world I saw as on her judgment day
when the war ends, and the sky rolls away,
and all is light, love and eternity.

Kathleen Raine

Ozymandias

I met a traveller from an antique land
Who said—'Two vast and trunkless legs of stone
Stand in the desert. Near them, on the sand,
Half sunk, a shattered visage lies, whose frown
And wrinkled lip, and sneer of cold command,
Tell that its sculptor well those passions read
Which yet survive, stamped on these lifeless things,
The hand that mocked them and the heart that fed;
And on the pedestal these words appear:
"My name is Ozymandias, King of Kings:
Look on my Works, ye Mighty, and despair!"
Nothing beside remains. Round the decay
Of that colossal Wreck, boundless and bare,
The lone and level sands stretch far away.'

Percy Bysshe Shelley

Ode to a Pythian Athlete

The delight of mortals grows in a moment,
and then falls to the ground,
shaken by adversity.
What is man? What is he not?
Frail being of a day,
uncertain shadow of a dream.
But when the light of heaven falls upon him
His life glows with joy.

ἐν δ' ὀλίγῳ βροτῶν
τὸ τερπνὸν αὔξεται: οὕτω δὲ καὶ πίτνει χαμαί,
ἀποτρόπῳ γνώμᾳ σεσεισμένον.
ἐπάμεροι: τί δέ τις; τί δ' οὔ τις; σκιᾶς ὄναρ
ἄνθρωπος. ἀλλ' ὅταν αἴγλα διόσδοτος ἔλθῃ,
λαμπρὸν φέγγος ἔπεστιν ἀνδρῶν καὶ μείλιχος αἰών.

from **Pindar**, Pythian Ode no. 8

Kneeling

Moments of great calm,
Kneeling before an altar
Of wood in a stone church
In summer, waiting for the God
To speak; the air a staircase
For silence; the sun's light
Ringing me, as though I acted
A great rôle. And the audiences
Still; all that close throng
Of spirits waiting, as I,
For the message.
                    Prompt me, God;
But not yet. When I speak,
Though it be you who speak
Through me, something is lost.
The meaning is in the waiting.

RS Thomas

Ode

Happy the man, and happy he alone,
He who can call today his own:
He who, secure within, can say,
Tomorrow do thy worst, for I have lived today.
 Be fair or foul or rain or shine
The joys I have possessed, in spite of fate, are mine.
Not Heaven itself upon the past has power,
But what has been, has been, and I have had my hour.

John Dryden, from an Ode by Horace

from Psalm 103

The Lord that made vs knoweth our shape,
Our mould and fashion iust;
How weake and frayle our nature is,
 And how we be but dust;

And how the tyme of mortall men
Is like the withering hay,
Or like the flower right fayre in field,
That fadeth full soone away:
Whose glosse and beauty stormy winds
Do vtterly disgrace,
And make that after their assaults
Such blossomes haue no place.

But yet the goodnesse of the Lord
With his shall euer stand;
Their children's children do receiue
His goodnesse at his hand:
I meane, which keepe his couenant
With all their whole desire,
And not forget to do the thing
That he doth them require.

Thomas Sternhold

Psalm 103

The Lord knows how we were made;
he remembers that we are dust.
As for mortals, their days are like grass;
they flourish like a flower of the field;
for the wind passes over it, and it is gone,
and its place knows it no more.
But the steadfast love of the Lord is
from everlasting to everlasting
on those who fear him,
and his righteousness to children's children,
those who keep his covenant
and remember to do his commandments.

In Broken Images

He is quick, thinking in clear images;
I am slow, thinking in broken images.

He becomes dull, trusting to his clear images;
I become sharp, mistrusting my broken images.

Trusting his images, he assumes their relevance;
Mistrusting my images, I question their relevance.

Assuming their relevance, he assumes the fact;
Questioning their relevance, I question the fact.

When the fact fails him, he questions his senses;
When the fact fails me, I approve my senses.

He continues quick and dull in his clear images;
I continue slow and sharp in my broken images.

He in a new confusion of his understanding;
I in a new understanding of my confusion.

Robert Graves

As we know

There are known knowns,
These are things we know that we know.

There are known unknowns,
that is to say
there are things that we know
we don't know.

But there are also
unknown unknowns
These are things
we don't know we don't know.

Donald Rumsfeld

Autumn

Why is that we want things sewn up
Neatly stacked in tied bundles
Waiting for the lighting of the autumn fire
Crisp leaves, sun dried grass cuttings, branches still bendy
Curled petal remains of dead roses

When really disorder is life
Unfinished, roughedged, and incomplete
And the bundles just metaphors
Lying waiting in piles
for children to scuff through the leaves
And, scattering, invent new thoughts?

Alison Morgan

Digging

Today I think
Only with scents – scents dead leaves yield,
And bracken, and wild carrot's seed,
And the square mustard field;
Odours that rise
When the spade wounds the roots of tree,
Rose, currant, raspberry, or goutweed,
Rhubarb or celery;
The smoke's smell, too,
Flowing from where a bonfire burns
The dead, the waste, the dangerous,
And all to sweetness turns.
It is enough
To smell, to crumble the dark earth,
While the robin sings over again
Sad songs of Autumn mirth.

Edward Thomas

BC: AD

This was the moment when Before
Turned into After, and the future's
Uninvented timekeepers presented arms.

This was the moment when nothing
Happened. Only dull peace
Sprawled boringly over the earth.

This was the moment when even energetic Romans
Could find nothing better to do
Than counting heads in remote provinces.

And this was the moment
When a few farm workers and three
Members of an obscure Persian sect

Walked haphazard by starlight straight
 Into the kingdom of heaven.

UA Fanthorpe

The Great Intruder

It is exasperating
to be called
so persistently
when the last thing
we want to do
is get up
and go
but God
elects
to keep on haunting
like some
holy ghost.

Thomas John Carlisle

The release

It was so still that day
and cold: the hills
brown shoulder to shoulder
seemed too old

to recall
when the slam of a hammer
on the vile nails
rang through those high lands

But suddenly
the sound ceased

and seamless as Christ's brown robe
all the leaves of the forest fell quietly;
and the injured one rose up
freed of his grave clothes.

John Crossley

Revenge

My personal revenge will be your children's
right to schooling and to flowers.
My personal revenge will be this song
bursting for you with no more fears.
My personal revenge will be to make you the goodness in my
        people's eyes,
implacable in combat always
generous and firm in victory.

My personal revenge will be to greet you 'Good morning!' in streets
with no beggar when instead of locking you inside
they say, 'Don't look so sad.'
When you, the torturer,
daren't lift your head.
My personal revenge will be to give you these hands you once
        ill-treated
with all their tenderness intact.

Luis Enrique Mejia Godoy

translated by Dinah Livingstone

Song based on words by Tomás Borge, addressed to his torturers when he was
in prison during the Somoza dictatorship in Nicaragua. After the triumph of
the Sandinista Revolution in 1979, Tomás became Interior Minister. He visited
his torturers, shook hands and forgave them. With his active support, the
Sandinistas abolished the death penalty. Tomás Borge died on 30th April 2012.
Luis Enrique can be heard singing the original song on YouTube. Google 'Luis
Enrique venganza personal'.

Paradise

I saw light running like a river
flashing, flowing between banks painted wlth spring.
Living sparks sprang from the torrent
diverting, dipping into the bright flowers
like rubies set in a circlet of gold.
Then, as if overpowered by strength of scent
the sparks plunged again into the deep current
entering, leaving, a constant exchange

As my eyes drank from the clear waters
suddenly the stretched water became round
and like people unmasked, flowers and sparks
became choirs of heaven, reflected like petals
in an amphitheatre formed in the shape of a golden rose.

And into the yellow depths of the eternal rose
dilating, turning, chanting a perfume of praise
to the springtime sun

Beatrice drew me.

Like one dreaming with open eyes
waking to find the feelings stamped on his soul
but the memory vanished, gone,
so was I; for when my vision ended, still
the sweet memory was distilled in my heart -
as when snow melts in the sun,
as wind scatters the brittle leaves on which
the Sibyl wrote her prophecy.

In those depths I saw,
bound with threads of love into a single volume
everything that is scattered through the universe;
substances, accidents, flowing together
into something like a simple light.

In the deep, clear substance of this light

I saw three arches, each of three colours
one reflected from another like rainbow from rainbow
and the third seemed like fire, breathed from the other two.

And in the centre of this light, painted in its colours
I saw the image of our own human form
I the mathematician struggling to reconcile
square and circle, and failing to find the formula;
I wanted to define the image within the circle
yet finding my mind, flightless, struck suddenly
by a flash of light and grace.

I fainted, overcome
but my mind and my heart were left turning
like a wheel in constant, even motion
powered by the love which moves the sun and other stars.

Dante Alighieri
adapted and translated by Alison Morgan from *Paradiso* XXX and XXXIII

Dante's final vision,
by Gustav Doré

On His Blindness

When I consider how my light is spent,
  Ere half my days, in this dark world and wide,
  And that one talent which is death to hide,
  Lodged with me useless, though my soul more bent
To serve therewith my maker, and present
  My true account, lest he returning chide,
  Doth God exact day-labour, light denied?
  I fondly ask; but Patience to prevent
That murmur, soon replies, God doth not need
  Either man's work or his own gifts, who best
  Bear his mild yoke, they serve him best, his state
Is kingly. Thousands at his bidding speed
  And post o'er land and ocean without rest:
  They also serve who only stand and wait.

John Milton

John Milton, by
Jonathan Richardson Jr,
1730-50

84

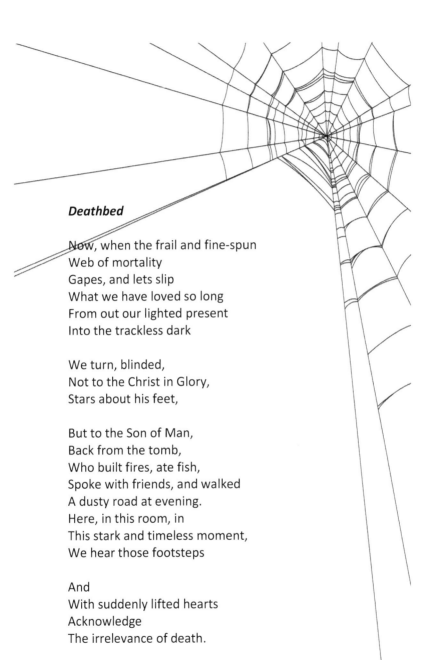

Deathbed

Now, when the frail and fine-spun
Web of mortality
Gapes, and lets slip
What we have loved so long
From out our lighted present
Into the trackless dark

We turn, blinded,
Not to the Christ in Glory,
Stars about his feet,

But to the Son of Man,
Back from the tomb,
Who built fires, ate fish,
Spoke with friends, and walked
A dusty road at evening.
Here, in this room, in
This stark and timeless moment,
We hear those footsteps

And
With suddenly lifted hearts
Acknowledge
The irrelevance of death.

Evangeline Paterson

Late Fragment

And did you get what
you wanted from this life, even so?
I did.
And what did you want?
To call myself beloved, to feel myself
beloved on the earth.

Raymond Carver

Before Sleep

The toil of day is ebbing,
The quiet comes again,
In slumber deep relaxing
The limbs of tired men.

And minds with anguish shaken,
And spirits racked with grief,
The cup of all forgetting
Have drunk and found relief.

The still Lethean waters
Now steal through every vein,
And men no more remember
The meaning of their pain....

Let, let the weary body
Lie sunk in slumber deep.
The heart shall still remember
Christ in its very sleep.

Prudentius

"I want to beg you... to be patient towards all that is unsolved in your heart and try to love *the questions themselves* like locked rooms and like books that are written in a very foreign tongue. Do not now seek the answers that cannot be given you because you would not be able to live them. And the point is, to live everything. *Live* the questions now. Perhaps you will then gradually, without noticing it, live along some distant day into the answer."

Rainer Maria Rilke

"A man has made at least a start on discovering the meaning of human life when he plants shady trees under which he knows full well he will never sit."

D Elton Trueblood

"The new one was a deeper country."

CS Lewis

Poetry acknowledgements

Works by the following are reproduced by kind permission of the authors or their representatives:

Dave Bookless – reproduced from *God Doesn't Do Waste* (IVP 2010)
Cesca Cavender – reproduced by permission of the author
Martin Cavender – reproduced by permission of the author
Carol Ann Duffy – reproduced by permission of the author
UA Fanthorpe – reproduced from *New and Collected Poems* (Enitharmon 2010) by permission of RV Bailey
Martyn Halsall – reproduced by permission of the author
Sophie Hannah – reproduced from *Leaving and Leaving You* (Carcanet Press 1999) by permission of the author
Elizabeth Jennings – reproduced from *New Collected Poems* (Carcanet Press 2002) by permission of David Higham Associates Ltd
Graham Kings – reproduced by permission of the author
Thelma Laycock – reproduced by permission of the author
John Leax – reproduced by permission of the author
Ann Lewin – reproduced from *Watching for the Kingfisher* (Canterbury Press 2009) by permission of the author
Roger McGough – reproduced by permission of the author
Alastair McIntosh – reproduced from *Love & Revolution* (Luath Press 2006) by permission of the author
Elma Mitchell – reproduced by permission of Harry Chambers
Alison Morgan – reproduced by permission of the author
Katy Morgan – reproduced by permission of the author
Ann Pilling – reproduced by permission of the author
Sheenagh Pugh – reproduced from *The Beautiful Lie* (Seren 2002) and *Later Collected Poems* (Seren 2009) by permission of the author
Henry Reed – extract from 'Lessons of the War' ' reproduced by permission of The Royal Literary Fund
Luci Shaw – used with the author's permission
Michael Swan – reproduced from *The Shapes of Things* (Oversteps Books 2011) by permission of the author
RS Thomas – © Kunjana Thomas 2001, reproduced from *Collected Poems 1945-1990* (Phoenix 2000)
Randall J VanderMey – reproduced by permission of the author
Rowan Williams – First Thing' © Rowan Williams 2002 appears in *The Poems of Rowan Williams* (Oxford: Perpetua Press and Grand Rapids, MI: Eerdmans) and is reproduced here by kind permission of Dr Williams and the Perpetua Press
Veronica Zundel – 'A Quiet Roar' was first published in the anthology *Faith in Her Words* (Lion Publishing 1991) and is reproduced by permission of the author

Works by the following are reproduced by kind permission of the publishers:

Simon Armitage – reproduced from *Kid* (2010) by permission of Faber & Faber
Raymond Carver – reproduced from *All of Us: Collected Poems* (Harvill Press 1997) by permission of The Random House Group
Eiléan ní Chuilleanáin – reproduced from *Selected Poems* (2008) by kind permission of the author and The Gallery Press
Thomas John Carlisle – reprinted by permission of the publisher (Eerdmans), all rights reserved
EE Cummings – ©1950, 1978, 1991 by the Trustees for the E.E. Cummings Trust. © 1979 by George James Firmage, from *Complete Poems 1904-1962* edited by George J Firmage. Used by permission of Liveright Publishing Corporation.
Cecil Day Lewis – reprinted by permission of Peters Fraser & Dunlop (www.petersfraserdunlop.com) on behalf of the Estate of C Day Lewis
Imtiaz Dharker – reproduced from *Leaving Fingerprints* (2009) by permission of Bloodaxe Books
Stephen Dunn – 'Happiness' is reproduced from *Between Angels* (1990) by kind permission of WW Norton & Co
Robert Frost – reproduced from *The Poetry of Robert Frost* (Vintage Classics 2013) by permission of The Random House Group
Robert Graves – reproduced from *Complete Poems in One Volume* (2000) by permission of Carcanet Press
Gerard Manley Hopkins – reproduced from *The Poems of Gerard Manley Hopkins 4E* edited by WH Gardner & NH MacKenzie (1970) by permission of Oxford University Press on behalf of The British Province of the Society of Jesus
P J Kavanagh – reproduced from *Kavanagh: Collected Poems* (1992) by permission of Carcanet Press
Philip Larkin – reproduced from *Collected Poems* (1988) by permission of Faber & Faber
Laurie Lee – reproduced from *Selected Poems* (Penguin 1985) by permission of Carol MacArthur of United Agents on behalf of the Laurie Lee estate
Norman MacCaig – poems reproduced from *The Poems of Norman McCaig* (Polygon 2009) by kind permission of Berlinn Books on behalf of the estate of Norman MacCaig
Sylvia Plath – reproduced from *Collected Poems* (2002) by permission of Faber & Faber
Ezra Pound – reproduced from *New Selected Poems and Translations* (2011) by permission of New Directions Publishing
Kathleen Raine – 'Passion' is reproduced from *The Collected Poems of Kathleen Raine* (Golgonooza Press 2000) by permission of Brian Keeble
Irina Ratushinskaya – reproduced by permission of Andrew Nurnberg Associates, © Irina Ratushinskaya 1986
Siegfried Sassoon – © Siegfried Sassoon by kind permission of the Estate of George Sassoon
E J Scovell – reproduced from *Collected Poems* (1988) by permission of Carcanet Press
William Stafford – reproduced from *The Way It Is: New and Selected Poems*, © 1970, 1998 by William Stafford and the Estate of William Stafford, by permission of The Permissions Company, Inc, on behalf of Graywolf Press, Minneapolis, Minnesota, www.graywolfpress.com
Wallace Stevens – reproduced from *Collected Poems* (2006) by permission of Faber & Faber

Anne Stevenson – reproduced from *Poems 1955-2005* by permission of Bloodaxe Books

Kit Wright – reproduced from *The Magic Box : poems for children* (2010) by permission of Macmillan Children's Books, London, UK

The following translations are reproduced by kind permission of their authors:

Dante Alighieri – Alison Morgan
Luis Enrique Mejia Godoy – Dinah Livingstone. 'Revenge' is published in bilingual text in *Poets of the Nicaraguan Revolution*, trans and ed Dinah Livingstone (Katabasis, London 1993).
Ann Griffiths – 'I saw him standing' (*translation from the Welsh of Ann Griffiths, 1776— 1805*) © Rowan Williams 1994 in *After Silent Centuries*; reproduced here by kind permission of Dr Williams and the Perpetua Press from *The Poems of Rowan Williams* (Oxford: Perpetua Press and Grand Rapids, MI: Eerdmans, 2002)
Eugenio Montale – John Richmond (www.myproperlife.com)
Pablo Neruda – Alison Morgan
Pindar – Alison Morgan

Works by the following are in the public domain and are freely available online and in published collections and anthologies:

W H Davies
Emily Dickinson
John Donne
John Dryden
James Elroy Flecker
Ivor Gurney
Thomas Hardy
George Herbert
Robert Herrick
John Keats
G A Studdert Kennedy
King James Bible
D H Lawrence
Henry Wadsworth Longfellow

John Gillespie Magee
John Milton
Charles Péguy
Prudentius
Donald Rumsfeld
William Shakespeare
Arthur O'Shaughnessy
Percy Bysshe Shelley
Thomas Sternhold
Sara Teasdale
Edward Thomas
William Wordsworth
W B Yeats

Image acknowledgements

Copyright for the following images belongs to the authors:

pp 21,24,25,27,28,47,73,76 © Alison Morgan
p 30 © Peter Clare | www.peterclare.co.uk
p 37 © Gabriel Vandervort | www.ancientresource.com
p 40 © Martin Cavender
p 44 © Posy Simmonds by permission of United Agents Ltd (www.unitedagents.co.uk) on behalf of the author
p 49 © Richard Bedford | www.richardbedford.co.uk
p 66 © D&B Militaria Ltd
p 84 © The Trustees of the British Museum

Reproduced under licence:

Cover image © dinostock, Fotolia.com
Fotolia.com : images on pp 12,13,14,16,19,20,29,33,37,41,43,44,45,46, 51,52,53,58,63,64,69,72,78,79,81
Istockphoto.com : images on pp 23,32,36,42,62,75,80,85
123RF.com : images on pp 22,70,71
Stockxpert.com : image on p 26
Microsoft : images on pp 18,50,68,70

Images on the following pages are in the public domain:

pp 39,48,55,56,74,83,84

For further reading

Details of published collections by contributing authors can be found in the acknowledgements above. Or try one of these anthologies:

Staying Alive, Being Alive, Being Human – three collections edited by Neil Astley and published by Bloodaxe Books (2002, 2004, 2011)
The Oxford Book of Twentieth Century English Verse, chosen by Philip Larkin (OUP 1973)
The Rattle Bag, edited by Seamus Heaney & Ted Hughes, Faber 1982
The Nation's Favourite... series of poetry published by the BBC
Poems on the Underground series, various publishers

ReSource publications

ReSource publishes a series of booklets on various aspects of the spiritual life, including:

Decision – an explanation of what is involved in becoming a Christian
Fasting – the forgotten gift, the neglected discipline
Knowing God's Love – a personal meditation
New in Christ – resources for personal renewal
Prayer Ministry
Praying with Creation
Renewal in Scripture
Who do you say that I am? The Unexpected Jesus
The Word of God – what does it mean?

ReSource also publishes a termly magazine which carries poetry, often previously unpublished, alongside articles, testimonies, book reviews, art and Bible reflections.

For more information on these and our other publications please visit www.resource-arm.net.

The editors

Martin Cavender is a former ecclesiastical lawyer, serving for many years as Diocesan Registrar for the Diocese of Bath and Wells. Martin was the Director of Springboard, the Archbishops' Initiative for Evangelism, and is now the Director of ReSource.

Alison Morgan is the author of *Dante and the Medieval Other World* (CUP 1990), *What Happens When We Die?* (Kingsway 1995), *The Wild Gospel* (Monarch 2005), *Doing What Jesus Did* (ReSource 2009) and *The Word on the Wind* (Monarch 2011). Formerly a university lecturer in Italian, Alison is an Anglican minister and works as a thinker and writer for ReSource.

ReSource is an independent charity based in Wells, Somerset. Our vision is to help build a church which is diverse, local, renewed in the Spirit and effective in mission. We work all over the UK and beyond – do visit our website for more information about what we offer.